Easy, Play-By-Numbers Piano Handbook

Easy, Play-By-Numbers Piano Handbook

(Pro-players' secrets)

Paula J. Tuttle
(aka: Paula ("PC") Douglas)

To order additional copies of this book, contact:
Xlibris Corporation
1-888-795-4274
www.Xlibris.com
Orders@Xlibris.com
60333

Contents

Prelude

(About the author)

Born in 1950 in Berea, Ohio (near Cleveland) my first love was animals, horses in particular, but ALL animals. My mom preferred to expose me to music via the piano, since she grew up in a musical family with a grand piano (but they also had horses!). Guess in the early 1900's horses were still necessary, so everyone had them, and cleaning barns was a reality she thought she'd spare me.

So, mom enrolled me in piano lessons at the Cleveland Institute of Music at the age of 7, and faithfully hauled me to them every Saturday morning, every summer, through my elementary school years. Piano lessons weren't exactly my favorite summer activity. I'd rather have been riding my bike or a horse than sitting at a piano learning how to read (what seemed like) meaningless symbols on a page. Even when I could translate the notes to the piano keys, I was just reading the notes off a piece of paper. Without the written notes in front of me, I couldn't play anything! I've never met sheet music which was actually written in a Key compatible with my alto vocal range. The system in this book teaches you how to make good use of that sheet music, by 'transposing' the Key/chords in that same sheet music to suit your voice!

In the 1970's I lived in a neighborhood in Hollywood where a lot of musicians lived. I met a piano player there whose name was Joey Carbone. Joey lived just 2 blocks from me, in a very sweet little house with the living room filled with a grand piano. He was a studio piano player in Hollywood, and was playing piano for the Righteous Brothers on tour at the time. What I found most fascinating, was that he had no formal training, and couldn't 'read' music! He began in New York as a bass-player, and now played the greatest Gospel-style piano I ever heard! I begged him to teach me how he did it, and he agreed. I rented a piano and practiced what he was teaching me for hours at a time. I couldn't tear myself away from my rented baby-grand!

In about 1974, I was playing guitar and singing in a restaurant in the San Fernando Valley, when an agent approached me, asking if I would audition for lead singer in a band he managed in Los Angeles. I was going by the name of "Paula Cooper (PC) Douglas" in those days.

The next thing I knew, the band and I were flying to Hawaii for a 6-week gig at a brand new hotel on Oahu's Waikiki Beach strip. I met and married my first husband there, also a singer, and from New Rochelle, New York. His name was Buddy Buono. Buddy and his older brother Bruce, had grown up in New York's 1950's and 1960's music scene. Bruce usually included Buddy in many of his musical endeavors and friendships. Bruce knew and briefly sang with "The Band" and "The Young Rascals", and occasionally played the conga drums. But mostly the brothers were phenomenal singers and music arrangers—not musicians.

Buddy wanted to promote me as an artist & songwriter, so he called an old friend, who had since graduated from Julliard and had become a famous New York guitar-player and music producer, David Spinozza. In their young years, David and Buddy had a little duo they called "Little Davie & Buddy". Buddy asked Dave if he would listen to me sing a couple of my songs. Dave agreed, and came to our place in Rye, NY. I was about 7 months pregnant at the time, but after dinner I performed 2 of the more recent Pop songs I'd written. Dave seemed pleasantly surprised, and set out to arrange my songs and hire musicians to make a demo. Within a couple of months, I wound up in Studio B of RCA records, making a demo with some of the best studio players in New York, and arrangements of my songs by David Spinozza. Dave's idea was to manage my career, but it was a project that would have to be worked on in Dave's spare time, which he had little of in those days. Buddy & I divorced before the project got going. But it sure was a great experience. I moved back to Cleveland with our new baby, Jesse.

I continued writing, mostly Country Songs back home in Cleveland, Ohio. By then, I had been practicing the 'numbers-method' in this book long enough that I got a Cleveland agent interested in booking club dates for me for the next 5 years. I played piano and guitar, accompanying the songs I sang . . . no longer needing sheet music.

In 1979, a Cleveland country radio station ran a regional country music contest for a National Barbara Mandrel songwriter contest. I won the Cleveland segment with a song I wrote called "Country Air". I didn't win the National contest, but a few years later, in 1985, I moved to Nashville anyway.

Nashville has some of the best back-up singers and studio players I've ever known. Like Joey Carbone, Nashville studio players primarily used the "numbers system" too, basically a very similar system Joey had taught me, which had no particular name at the time. I spent 4 years in Nashville, lucky enough to meet many of Nashville's finest players, which resulted in the best part of being in Nashville . . . improving my playing, writing and singing, thanks to great input from great & talented people.

In 1991, the music hadn't lost any luster, but the 'business' of it had. I was horrible at business, and had no one to handle that part for me. So, I bought a 6-month old Morgan colt in Huntsville, Alabama and Jesse & I hauled "Arthur" back home to Cleveland. It was time to finally pursue my childhood dream of owning a horse and learning everything I could about them. So I purchased a 10-acre farm in Medina, Ohio where Amish buggies streamed by the place in the morning and late afternoon . . . we called these times "Amish rush-hour". Since 1993, music has remained a wonderful hobby. I decided to write this book because I know there are many aspiring musicians out there who either can't play an instrument at all, or like me, can only read music. Folks who can't "jamm" with other musicians or just sit down at a piano and play without their sheet music.

I sold the farm in 1996 and moved to horse country in northern New Mexico. Although I spend most of my time these days riding and driving Arthur through the New Mexico countryside, I keep my guitar and my family's grand piano in the living room, and teach this method to friends and children who want to learn. Please enjoy!

Chapter 1

Music is a language
Of its own

The phrase "playing-by-ear" really means a person doesn't need to read a song from sheet-music, because they understand the basic reasoning & simple math behind how & why music works.

To demonstrate another advantage of this simple music system begs the question, "how often does someone at a birthday party start Happy Birthday too high or too low for you?" There is a comfortable "Key" that would allow you to comfortably sing any particular song within a range of notes that lend themselves to your particular voice. Seems like no one ever starts off Happy Birthday in that one!

Another person with a higher or lower voice range would have to sing the same song in a different "Key" in order to be comfortable singing it. There are a total of 12 "Keys" (range of notes/scales) in which a song can be played or sung to suit ANY vocal range! This applies to all musical instruments, not just the piano.

Music is a language of it's own. Like any language, the best way to learn it is to learn how to **speak/comprehend** it before learning to write it. Here, you will learn primarily how to speak the language of music.

Once you can actually play songs by the method in this book, learning to read sheet-music will come easier too (if you choose to do so).

Note: The study of formally-taught music theory is a complex field in its entirety, but a short-cut to the basics are really what you're learning from this book. I took a college-level Music Theory course once, and concluded that it complicated it's own basic simplicity! It was more confusing than inspiring! With this easy method, there is no end to how far you can go in the music field, and I encourage you to take the journey as far as possible! Now, let's get started seeing how it works!

Example of this number-system's application

A band musician, teaching a song to his/her band might say: "In Key of E, play the I, IV and V chords for the first 8 bars." When the pattern changes, the leader will call out the alternate chords by number as well. If the leader were to write the song out for the players, he/she would put the name of the Key at the top of the page, (ie: "Key of C" or "Key of D", etc) then notate all the chords in their proper order with Roman Numerals. No matter what Key the song will be played in, the same chord progression will still be depicted the same way: "I, IV, V chords", etc. The music arranger seldom needs to name notes or chords like "play a C-chord", play a D-chord", for the band because **the chord-numbers are the same in *any* Key.** You'll soon see . . . it's all 'relative'.

THE PIANO SAYS IT BEST

(A quick note on a common misnomer): The piano is not a stringed instrument . . . it is a percussion instrument . . . because 'hammers' ***strike*** the keys).

- **There are only 12 notes on the piano** . . . *they just keep repeating.*

They consist of: *7 white notes*—A, B, C, D, E, F, G—and *5 black notes* which just keep repeating from one end of the instrument to the other! The black notes are the flats(b) and sharps(#) corresponding to the white notes adjoining them. Black note is "flat(b)" if it's located on the left of a white note, and is "sharp(#)" if located to the right of a white note. There you have it . . . the entire musician's tool-kit! With these tools, the possibilities are virtually endless!!

The black & white notes form an obvious pattern throughout the keyboard: 3 black notes, 2 black notes, 3 black notes, 2 black notes, etc. The same is true of ALL instruments but only the piano/keyboard visually demonstrates this fact!

If you don't have a piano, any type of keyboard will suffice to learn what's taught here, augmented by the illustrations and exhibits toward the back of the book.

Please check out the Illustrations of a keyboards Exhibit (36), as we begin to talk about **Scales**.

This book consists of a number of **"Formulas"** for applying the 12 existing notes to any of 12 possible "Keys".

The formulas for making a Chromatic Scale and a Major Scale are on the following few pages, and must be well-understood before you can begin to build a broader understanding of how music works and how playing by numbers works. Scales lay the foundation for the whole system.

ROOT NOTES & "KEYS":

The **first note** of a scale is the "**root note**". It's the note you choose to start a scale. The Root-note is also the **name of that scale**, and therefore, the name of the particular "Key" you'll be playing and/or singing a song in. So with only 12 possible notes to play, there are only 12 different possible "Keys" to play a song in!

"**Key**" (upper-case K) is a term for describing the scale of notes within which a particular song will be played, that best suit's a particular singer's voice. By determining the "Key" the song is in, you're communicating what notes & chords that will be played.

As you start to learn how to make chords, the names of the chords will ALSO be taken from the name of the root-note of that chord. For example, the root note of a D-chord is a "D-note".

As you probably know, the black & white notes on the piano are *also* called "keys". So, to avoid confusion, we'll use lower-case "**key**" when we're talking about actual piano notes, and upper case "**Key**" for a song's scale of notes/vocal range.

Review

Only 12 notes exist, there are only 12 possible scales, and there are only 12 possible Keys to play in. They just keep repeating throughout the instrument, so you can play any particular song in any vocal range. The formulas taught in this book apply to making ANY of 12 Scales or chords in any of 12 Keys. In other words, once you learn the formula for making a scale in the Key of C, the formula's is the same for all the other scales beginning on any of 12 **Root-notes.**

Chapter 2

Scales:

"Scale" defined: **"An ascending or descending series of musical tones, proceeding in accordance with a specified scheme of intervals"** (Webster's II).

First, white notes have alphabetical names: A, B, C, D, E, F, G, (A) . . . . Black notes are "flats(b)" and "sharps(#)" of the white notes. Examples: A#, Eb, F#, Db, etc . . . . Much more on this later.

"Chromatic scale" (a scale of all ½-steps):

The piano keys are all a ½-step from each other. Pick ANY note on the piano . . . call that note your **root-note** (first note) of the scale you'll be playing and therefore will name the scale too. Then, play 13 consecutive notes to either the right or left of that original note. *The 13th note will be the **same** note you started on,* ending that scale and beginning the next, **same scale**, going higher or lower.

You've played a "**Chromatic Scale**", *a scale of ½-steps*. If you started the scale on (say) a C-note and played a total of 13 consecutive notes, you've played a Chromatic Scale in "C". A Chromatic Scale demonstrates and includes all the possible 12 individual notes in existence.

*"**Major scale**" (a scale of whole-steps & ½-steps):* (please read the following paragraph very carefully)

By playing every OTHER note you've played a "whole-step". A Major scale will consist of 8 notes (1 and 8 are same note, an octave apart). In the C-Scale, every black note you skipped was a ½-step between the white notes you DID play. The result was that you played 5 whole-steps and two ½-steps from C to C playing only white notes consecutively. We'll delve into the Major scale deeper in just a bit, but for now I'll just say, the same formula will apply to ALL Major scales. For now, we're just building a foundation for the up-coming formulas involved in playing any song in any Key!

Octaves:

1 octave of a Chromatic Scale in C: C, C#, D, D#, E, F, F#, G, G#, A, A#, B, C

(ascending—left to right 1, 2, 3, 4, 5, 6, 7, 8, 9, 10, 11, 12, 13)

(*Every* note between C and C)

1 octave of a Major Scale in C: C, D, E, F, G, A, B, C (E to F is a ½ step

(ascending—left to right) 1, 2, 3, 4, 5, 6, 7, 8 B to C is a ½ step)

(*5 whole-steps, two ½-steps*)

Each time a pattern of 13 black & white notes repeats, the 13th note begins another *octave* **of that same scale—it's the same note as the 1st. Again, there are only 12 possible notes in existence! They just repeat. No matter what note you begin a scale on, the note you start & end on (the root-notes) will define the name of your scale.**

"Keys" (as applied to vocal ranges)

There are names for different voice ranges:

For women: **Soprano** *(high vocal range)*
           Alto *(mid to low vocal range)*
For men: **Tenor***(high vocal range)*
           Bass *(mid to low vocal range)*

There are additional terms used as well, but the point is that singers must sing in the "Key" that is most comfortable for their singing voice.

"Transposing":

Changing the Key that (say) a song was written in, to a Key that is more comfortable for your vocal range is called **transposing**. With the method in this book, transposing a song from (say) the Key of C to any other Key, is a simple matter of applying the same 'formulas' for making chords in the Key of C to any other Key you choose. It's all **"relative"**.

Music is actually based on simple math. The alphabetic note-names and chord-names may change, but **by *numbering* the notes** (1 thru 12) **& chords** (in roman numerals), all remains completely "relative" in ANY Key. You'll soon see how the Number-System simplifies things. No matter what Key you play a song in, by using terms like "the One chord ", "the Four chord", or "the Five chord", etc, it won't matter what Key you're in! Again, it's all relative! But I'm getting a little ahead of myself.

FORMULA(s)
Major Scales (7+1=8) notes

Major Scale:

The Major scales consist of only 7 different notes within the 12 total different notes in a Chromatic scale (a scale of all ½-steps) Note 13 repeats note 1. In a Major scale, note 8 is the same note as the first note for a total of 8 notes in the Major Scale. A Major scale consists of 5 whole-steps and two ½-steps = 8 total notes in a Major scale. But once you play the 1st note, where are the whole-steps and where are the ½-steps??

The following is the Formula for a Major Scale. Every "(and)" is a ½-step note you'll *skip*, so the "whole steps" are from notes 1 to 2, notes 2 to 3, notes 4 to 5, notes 5 to 6 and notes 6 to 7. The two ½-steps are notes 3 to 4 and 7 to 8. Again, there will be 5 whole-steps and 2 half-steps as you see here, in the same order in EVERY Major-scale:

1 (and) 2 (and) 3, 4 (and) 5 (and) 6 (and) 7, 8.

Major Scales will *always* sound like this:

DO, RE, MI, FA, SO, LA, TI, DO
(familiar?)

- You'll need to go to your piano, or have the "Major Scale" keyboard illustration in the back of this book handy for most of the rest of the book.
- The first Major scale to learn should be the "**C** Major Scale" because all 8 notes are white ones (no sharps or flats). Begin with the C-note in about the **middle** of the keyboard. **C** is **any white note to the immediate left of any set of 2-black notes.** The one in the middle of the keyboard is actually called "middle-C"! *Play every consecutive white note* to the next C-note and you'll have played 1

octave of the notes in a Major-C scale. Every 'run' of notes to the next C-note is another octave of a Major-C scale.

	One octave		*2ⁿᵈ octave*
2 octaves of a C Major scale:	*C* D E F G A B *C* D E F G A B *C*		

<———————|——————>

It's not that the black-notes are scary, they're just sharps (#) and flats (*b*) which come into play in *every* Key when playing songs. But again, for learning the Formula for a Major scale, I chose the Key of C to begin with because being all consecutive white notes, the whole-steps and ½-steps are most graphically demonstrated. The Major scale in any Key other than C will include up to 5 sharps(#) and/or flats(b). As you'll soon see, only the white notes have names from A to G, and the black notes take on the names "sharps" & "flats" of the white note on either side of them.

Fingers to use: As you play major scales, use your fingers in the following order:

Thumb plays #1, index finger #2, middle finger #3, **bring thumb under the palm and hit #4 with the thumb**, #5 with index, #6 with middle, #7 with ring finger, #8 with pinky. This order of fingers was figured out by someone who wanted to be able to end the scale with the pinky, and play it as smoothly as possible! Once you've practiced Major scales for awhile, you'll not only realize the truth of this, but it will carry over to all of your playing. It's like typing . . . if you "hunt & peck" you're typing is slow and choppy. If you learn the method they teach you in classes, and practice, you can get to where you're typing 60-120 words per minute!!

Left-Hand going left (lower): Start with thumb of left hand on note #1, index finger on note #2, middle finger on #3, **cross under with thumb to #4**, index on #5, middle on #6, ring finger on #7, pinky on #8. It will get smoother and faster with practice!

The C Major scale—same Formula, leaving out the ("and")s: *going right (ascending):*

Starting on middle C, it's a whole-step to D
From D, it's a whole-step to E
From E, it's a half-step to F
From F. it's a whole step to G
From G, it's a whole-step to A
From A, it's a whole-step to B
From B, it's a half-step to the final C

Knowing now that you're playing a C-major scale, let's give each note a number from 1 to 8, C=1, D=2, etc. If your root note/scale were in the Key of E (say), you would number the notes the same way, E=1, F#=2, G#=3, etc. The names of notes and Keys/scales change, but the numbers don't! (Refer anytime to the Tables in back of book for notes & chords—names & numbers).

Starting on middle C **going left (descending)***:*

Starting on middle C, it's a half-step to B
From B, it's a whole-step to A
From A, it's a whole-step to G
From G, it's a whole step to F
From F, it's a half-step to E
From E, it's a whole-step to D
From D, it's a whole-step to C

It's the same 'formula' no matter what note you begin on, to play any scale . . . the half and whole steps fall in the same order as in the Key of C. All 11 others will include between 1 and 6 sharps(#) and/or flats(b).

Study this little whole-step/half-step formula for other major-scales **by beginning** on any of the other 11 possible notes.

Formula(s) For
MAKING CHORDS

By now understanding what ½-steps & whole-steps are, and the Formula for making any Major scale, you're closer to understanding the formula for making **chords** within a Major scale of notes that best suits your voice—the **Key** you want to sing and/or play a song in.

Each Major **chord** consists of **3 basic/primary notes**. When played together at the same time with 3 fingers, a "chord" is played. In many ways, music is like art—music too has 3 Primary Colors from which all other colors stem, but in Music they're called Primary Chords instead of Primary Colors. Just like in the actual color chart/spectrum, the Primary colors are red, yellow & blue. In Music, these are the "I" chord, "IV" chord, and "V" chord. These numbers are based on the **root notes** of each of these 3 chords as in the following example:

For instance, in the Key of C the I, IV and V chords are a C-chord, F-chord and G-chord (aka: the 1-note, 4-note and 5-note in a C-Major scale). The root note in the Key of C is "C", so the I-Chord is a "C-chord". The 4th note in a C Major scale is F, so the IV chord is "F". The 5th note in the C Major scale is G, so the V chord is "G". It's the same 1, 4 & 5 notes which are the root notes of the 3-major chords in ANY Key!

Formula for making a Major chord:

Notes in ALL major chords: **"1", "3" and "5"** . . . **from the root note of the chord: root note + 2 whole steps to the "3" note, + 1 whole step & ½ step to the 5-note.** The notes for the I-chord (C-chord) will be: C, E & G. The IV-chord is F so, the root note (1) of the chord is F, the 3-note is A, and the 5th note is C. You can play the notes in any order you like the sound of, but for starters it's easiest to stay with this successive order.

Fingers to use for chords: Place your **thumb** on the C (root) note, place the **index finger** 2 'whole-steps' away (E), then count 1 'whole-step' + ½-step to the **ring-finger** note (G). Do the same for the IV-chord (F, A, C) and the V-chord (G, B, D).

Reminder:

A band musician, teaching a song to his/her band might say: "In Key of E, play the I, IV and V chords for the first 8 bars." When the chords change, the leader will call out the alternate chords by numbers from I to VII. If the leader were to write the song out for the players, he/she would place the name of the Key at the top of the page (Ex: Key of D, or Key of A-flat etc), then will notate all the chords in their proper order with Roman Numerals

In the Number System we will refer to individual *notes* by numbers (1, 2, 3, etc), and to *chords* by Roman-Numerals (I, II, III, IV, V, etc) to avoid confusion when discussing one or the other. Having said that, let's make chords!

Still in the key of C, the table below shows the "1", "3", and "5" notes simultaneously for all 7 possible Major chords in any Key.

The I-chord: **C, E, G.** *(primary chord)*
The II-chord: **D, F#, A** *(F# is the black note to the immediate right of the F-note)*
The III-chord: **E, G#, B** *(G# is the black note to the immediate right of the G-note)*
The IV-chord: **F, A, C** *(primary chord)*
The V-chord: **G, B, D** *(primary chord)*
The VI-chord: **A, C#, F** *(C# is the black note to the immediate right of the C-note)*
The VII-chord: **B, D#, F#** *(you now probably get the idea)*

- **You've just played all the Major chords in the Key of C.** No matter what Key is most comfortable for your voice, you can play a lot of Country songs just with the I, IV and V chords. The order in which you play each of these 3 chords will depend on the song's melody. You'll need to "sound-it-out" by ear.

Making "Minor" and "Seventh" Chords

1) *Important terms*:

    - *"Raising"* a note—This means to replace a particular note with another note a ½-step or whole-step **higher**.
    - *"Lowering"* a note—This means to replace a particular note with another note a ½-step or whole-step **lower**.

2) *Minor Chord* (*"lowering the 3rd"* ½ step):

    Now that you're familiar with making the I, IV and V chords in any Key, and that the NOTES in a Major-chord are the 1, 3 and 5 notes from the root note of the chord, by "lowering the 3rd" ½-step, you make a 'minor' from the Major chord.

    Example: In the Key of "C": The 1-Chord consists of the notes C, E and G. The "third" is the E-note. To make a **C-minor chord**, "lower" the 3rd (E) ½-step which is an E-flat. That's it! The other 2 notes (1/C and 5/G) don't change. Try it and hear the sound of a "C-minor" chord. A C-minor is written **Cm.**

3) **Minor 7th Chord** (*"lower* the 1/C (*root*) note *and* 3rd/E a **½-step each**): A **Cm7** chord consists of the notes: B, E-flat, F (add B "on-top "/pinky, if desired)

4) **Major 7th Chord**: (*"Lower"* the Root-Note a **whole-step**). A C7th chord is **written C7,** and consists of the notes: B-flat, E and G. **Only the root-note changed.**

These chords are the ones most used in Pop, Country, Rock & Blues. However, there are many other types of chords, many you'll discover as you 'play' with the chord combinations, and find yourself stumbling onto pleasant chord-changes and note-changes within your chords. That's the whole beauty of any "Art" . . . experimenting with the tools you have. Maybe writing your own songs!

The left hand plays the bass-clef of the piano—the notes in left half of the keyboard; Right-hand . . . middle to higher notes . . . right half of the keyboard. By experimenting with your songs, playing notes with your left-hand from your chords being played with the right-hand, you can get rhythms going in any way/sound you like and fills out the total sound. Once you find the chords to your song with your right hand (right of Middle-C), you could strike the *root*-note of each chord with a finger of your LEFT hand in the lower octaves (left of Middle-C). You'll at least have added a small additional dimension to the sound of each chord. If your fingers can reach, try placing your thumb on a bass root-note, and your pinky 1-octave to the left/lower, striking those 2 notes as you play the corresponding chord with your right hand. If you're coordinated enough, you can play the full chord with the both your left & right hands . . . or any combination of left-end notes from your right-end chords, played in any suitable rhythm you choose!

As you can see, all chords are branches off a Major-chord, and can be altered in many ways. When you're asked to **"raise"** a note, it means to replace one note with one a ½-step OR whole-step **higher** than the note in the Major-Chord (depending on what chord you're making). When you're asked to **"lower"** a note, it means to play the note a ½-step OR whole-step **lower** than the original note in the Major-Chord.

You've now learned the 'Formula' for making the following 5 types of chords:

1) Major Chord
2) Minor Chord
3) Major 7th Chord
4) Minor 7th Chord

Please enjoy practicing what you've learned to this point before going much further.

Suggestion: choose a few simple, familiar songs and find the scale of notes which are most comfortable for your voice, (finding your "Key"). Then, find the 3 Major chords within that Key. Don't forget to add at least the 1-finger root note of each chord in the bass-clef (octaves LEFT of Middle-C) for each chord played. At this point you've grasped the basics. You're beginning to understand and actually play simple songs by the number system.

"Filling out a chord":

This means you can add a 4th note (and others that compliment the chord) to 'fill it out'. This one's simple: by adding the root note one octave from the lower one, with your right-hand pinky, (aka **'top' of the chord—the 8-note**). For instance, if playing a C-chord (notes C, E, G, C), you'll get a noticeably 'fuller' chord. You're thumb is on the lowest end of the C-octave and your pinky is playing the C-note at the "top" of the Octave. You can practice 'filling out' all major-chords this way.

Chord Inversions:

Not to complicate matters, but I think it's important at this point to let you know that you can play the notes of a chord in any order too. For instance, in the Key of C (say), as long as you play the basic 3 notes (the 1, 3 and 5 notes) of the I, IV and V chords, instead of placing the thumb on the root note, you could place your thumb on the 3rd or the 5th and the ring or pinky finger on the root-note. You're still playing the same 3 notes in the chord, just in a different order. You'll be surprised, that even though you're playing the same 3 Major notes in the chord, by 'inverting' them, you'll get a slightly different sound. You can do the same with the IV and V chords, and with ANY chords for that matter! It all depends on the sound you like best for your song. Some songs will require the order—V, I, IV chords instead of I, IV and V. They can be 'inverted' to suit any song.

Practice Song (In the Key of D)

I used this song since most of you will know the melody and beats in this one, so applying the I, IV and V chords to the words & beat of the song should come fairly easily. I'm only giving you the 1st line of the song for several Keys, to show how Transposing a song from 1 Key to another only changes the alphabetical chord names, but not the chord numbers!

"When Will I Be Loved"

In the Key of D: (the actual name of the chords are above the Roman Numbers)

```
D       G  A  D     G  A  D      G    A    D
I       IV V  I     IV V  I      IV   V    I
```
"I've been chea-ted, been mi-strea-ted, When Will I—I Be Loved?"

In the Key of A:

```
A       D  E  A     D  E  A      D    E    A
I       IV V  I     IV V  I      IV   V    I
```
"I've been chea-ted, been mi-strea-ted, When Will I—I Be Loved?"

In the Key of G:
```
G       C  D  G     C  D  G      C    D    G
I       IV V  I     IV V  I      IV   V    I
```
"I've been chea-ted, been mi-strea-ted, When Will I—I Be Loved?"

If we played this song in the **Key of C**, the **I-chord will be a C-chord, the IV chord will be an F-chord and the V-chord will be a G-chord.**

Keep practicing this, one line at a time, with other simple songs. If you have trouble, go to the "Table of Chords", look for the Key you want to play the song in, and you'll see the I, IV and V chords. It's best to determine them by applying the Formula to get used to thinking that way. You can also refer back to the '**Formula' for making chords**.

Writing the Roman-Numeral chord names when they're Major, minor, etc:

Examples:

1) I chord: I7 (I 7th chord)
                Im7 (I minor 7th chord)
2) IV chord: IV7 (IV 7th chord)
                IVm7 (IV minor 7th chord)
3) V chord: V7 (V 7th chord)
                Vm7 (V minor 7th chord)

Chapter 3

Tempos/Rhythms:

When you tap your foot to the beat of a song, you are "keeping time" to the music. If you've noticed, in a band, the drums and bass-guitar players keep the beat to the song going, setting the "tempo". When you are alone at your piano, you'll have to be the whole band! The fingers of your left-hand will be playing chords or single notes in a rhythm, however best compliments the chords you're playing in contrast with your right-hand, which typically plays the melody OR chords, which support the melody if your singing.

The 'bass-clef' is typically notes to the left of Middle-C note, and the 'treble-clef' are the notes to the right of Middle-C. For starters, while playing (say) the I, IV and V chords in the Key of C in the 'treble-clef', (chords C, F and G), find the root-note of each chords in the 'bass-clef'. For instance, hit a C-note somewhere in the bass-clef, then play the C-chord somewhere in the treble-clef. Next, find the F-note in the 'base clef', play it with your left hand, and play the F-chord in the 'treble-clef' with your right hand. Do the same with the G note in the bass-clef and G-chord in the treble-clef.

Next, try playing the root-note in the bass-clef at the same time as you play the corresponding chord in the treble-clef.

Experiment with different ways of playing the root-note in the bass-clef with any chords you choose, played with your right-hand (in the treble-clef).

Also, practice JUST left-hand work, playing (say) the C, F and D individual notes in succession to the right, then back to the left. Try to create different rhythms doing this, and try it with the notes of lots of different chords! When you add your right-hand chords to the beat you're setting with the left-hand, experiment with lots of different moments to strike your right-hand chords. For instance, keep a steady, even beat with the left-hand notes, then, add the right-hand full chords at various intervals until a good beat emerges using both hands. At first, it will seem like you're patting your head and rubbing your belly! But you'll develop coordination eventually, if you practice.

Music is artistic expression, so express yourself and experiment away!

Playing with the Left-Hand (Bass clef):

Bass & Treble "Clefs": (Terms for communicating written music).

"Middle C" basically marks the middle of the piano. The "Treble Clef" is to the right of Middle-C, played with your right-hand (most of the time), and the "Base Clef" begins to the left of Middle-C with your left hand. The "Base Clef" is typically used for setting the "beat" of the song. So, your left-hand will be 'playing the bass', and your right-hand will be following the beats and basically playing the melody either with notes, chords and/or both.

I've included 2 stanzas of treble-clef (upper portion) and bass-clef (lower portion) blank staff paper. You can buy sheets of music staff paper by the pack, and/or notebooks of it inexpensively. It's good to have in case you want to transpose sheet music for a song into a different Key. It's also used by composers to write their music.

Chapter 4

Song Construction
(writing your own songs)

I thought it might be interesting to include this section in the book, for those who would like to write a song. There are certain tried & true ways to put a song together, that make great songs. It's called **"Mapping" the song** (where to put the verses, choruses, bridge and 'break'—(where there's only music, no vocal).

Parts of a song:

A song is really a poem put to music. Unlike the 2-3 hours it takes to tell a story in a movie, or the hundreds of pages in a book, a song should tell the whole story in 2-3 minutes! That means the #1 important thing is to select the best & least words possible, that quickly tell your whole story! Music & words together, make your story most memorable. Consider the mood of your song, and choose music that suits that mood.

Components of song-construction formulas are:

Chorus: Also known as the "hook" of a song, and generally the most memorable and repetitive within the song.

Verse: This is the Part of the song which 'sets-up' the story-line and leads into the Chorus.

Bridge: This is the portion of a song where the melody departs from the Verse & Chorus melodies. It is often shorter than a Verse or Chorus, and more or less breaks the monotony, adds heightened interest to the story, and keeps the song from becoming monotonous.

Examples of a few ways of "Mapping" a song:

Type I: Verse, Chorus, Verse, Bridge, Verse, Chorus
Type II: Chorus, Verse, Chorus, Bridge, Chorus
Type III: Verse, Chorus, Bridge, Verse, Chorus

These are just a few types of "maps" you can use to arrange the parts of your song. Most songs include a music-only solo, and can happen between where ever it sounds best to you . . . after the 2nd chorus is pretty typical, but there really aren't any hard & fast rules. Only 'formulas' that result in an interesting work.

Time-Signatures:

Time signatures give musical pieces their "feel". Ever hear the phrase "(so-many) beats per measure"? "Measures" consist of beats within each measure, and follow a pattern throughout any particular song. There are songs written in an array of Time-Signatures, the most common are:

- 4/4-time (four-four time) is most universal and typical time signature in Country Songs, Blues, and Pop music, and means "play 4-beats per measure".
- ¾-(three-quarter time) gives the Waltz it's 'feel'.
- 2/4-time (half-time) is a variation on 4/4-time, and is interesting. It means alternating "2-beats in a measure, then 4 beats in the next measure". Used often in Blues, Pop and Country music too.

Jazz is played in wide variety of Time-Signatures. I'm not a jazz-player, so I won't attempt to explain it! But, it's the different time-signatures that give jazz it's wide variety of 'feels'.

Time-signatures are included within all written music, in order to communicate the beat/rhythm of a song. Notes within each 'measure' in written music, are written as 'whole-notes', 'half-notes', 'quarter-notes', eighth-notes sixteenth-notes, etc, and, combined with the time-signature, measures and individual notes, tell the musician the melody, beat, and 'feel' of the music. A good sight-reader can play a song just like the recording of it, even if the musician has NEVER heard the song, just by reading the music! I just threw this in to give you an idea of what it takes to learn how to read music . . . a lot more intricate than the Numbers method!

Learning to read music is a very important skill for a musician to possess, especially for Classical and Jazz, which are modes of music almost always played by musicians who read music.

However, for those primarily interested in playing music to sing to, the number system allows and frees you to back up yours and/or another's singing in any Key desired. Otherwise, you're just copying notes off a page, without really understanding *why*. You can become fully dependant on sheet-music. When you don't have it, you just won't be able to play anything. What you're learning in this book is a simplified version of Music Theory.

Example of 4/4 (four-four) time within 2 measures:

Let's try here, to get a "feel" for counting measures. Here are 2 typical 4/4 measures.

```
_____ measure _____measure _____
|4__1___2___3___4 ____ | __1__2___3___4 ___|
|4 _____ |_____|
| _____ |_____|
| _____ |_____|
```

The 2 measures below are in ¾ **time—Waltz:**

```
_____ measure _____measure _____
|3_____1___2__ 3 _____ | ____1___2__ 3_____|
|4 _____ |_____|
| _____ |_____|
| _____ |_____|
| _____ |_____|
```

If we were to put notes on the above 'stanzas', each note's written style would depict the beats in and of themselves, resulting in 4-beats per measure or 3 beats per measure.

Table of all 12 Major Chords

No matter what Key you're playing a song in, you'll need to play at least 3 of the following Chords within that Key. Every Major Chord possible is below, along with the 1, 3, 5 notes in each particular Chord. The notes in parentheses are the **same notes** as the flats instead of sharps or sharps instead of flats, depending on the Key you're playing in:

Name of All Major Chords	3 Notes within major chord
"A" Chord	A, C#, E
B-flat (also A#) Chord	B-flat, D, F (A#, D, F)
B Chord	B, E-flat, G-flat
C Chord	C, E, G
C# (also D flat) Chord	C#, F, G# (D flat, F, A flat)
D Chord	D, F#, A
E-flat (also D#) Chord	E-flat, G, B-flat (D#, G, A#)
F Chord	F, A, C
F# (also G flat) Chord	F#, A#, C# (G flat, B flat, D flat)
G Chord	G, B, D
A-flat (also G#) Chord	A-flat, C, E-flat (G#, C, D#)

GRAND FINALE

The formulas and content in this handbook are typically used by professional studio and stage musicians. Some thought that naming the book "Play-By-Numbers" sounded like a children's book. That was just fine with me, because this handbook is simply aimed at teaching music in it's most basic simplicity for both children and adults.

This handbook did not need to be filled with hundreds of pages . . . all the tools needed to begin and grow your journey into becoming a musician easily fit into this tiny book! Now, with the Number-System formulas in your toolbox, you're empowered to practice and experiment to your heart's content!

As you apply this system to your daily practice-sessions, create new chord progressions and melodies, it will all gradually become automatic. With regular practice, you will become 'fluent' in the language of music, just as conversation in a foreign language becomes fluent with practice and persistence. With consistent use and practice, fluency will result!

I've enjoyed sharing the knowledge with you which set me off on an enjoyable career and adventure in the music world. Until I learned the 'numbers-system' and could only read music, I could not make a living playing for the public. Once the sheet music was no longer necessary, I was finally having fun, writing and playing my own songs and my favorite popular songs in any Key and style I chose!

I end this journey with you as you begin yours, saying "thank you" for your interest and purchase of my book, and may your musical journey be as magical and addictive as it was for me!

Paula J. Tuttle
Aka P.C. Douglas
e-mail: paulacooper.douglas@gmail.com

Keyboard Exhibits

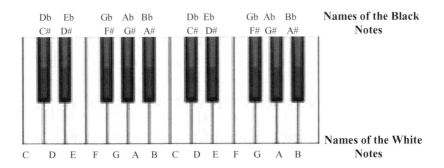

Names of the Black Notes

Names of the White Notes

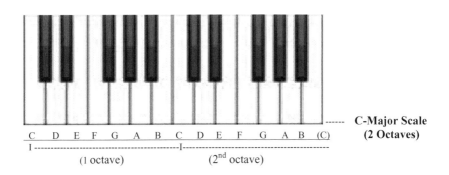

C-Major Scale (2 Octaves)

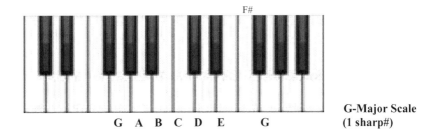

G-Major Scale (1 sharp#)

Quick Referrence Guide

Table of 11 Major Chords

Name of Chord	*1st,3rd, 5th*
A	A, C#, E
Bb (aka A#)	Bb, D, F (A#, D, F)
B	B, Eb, Gb
C	C, E, G
C# (aka Db)	C#, F, G# (Db, F, Ab)
D	D, F#, A
D# (aka Eb)	D#, G, A# (Eb, G, Bb)
F	F, A, C
F# (aka Gb)	F#, A#, C# (Gb, Bb, Db)
G	G, B, D
G# (aka Ab)	G#, C, D# (Ab, C, Eb)

Table of All Major Chords
(in all possible Keys)

Major Chords in:

Key of "A" (notes 1st, 3rd & 5th)

		Major Scale of Key
		Sharps(#) and Flats(b)
		in I, IV, V chords and Major scales

I Chord: A, C#, E
II Chord: B, D#, F#
III Chord: C#, F, G#   A, B, C#, D, E F#, G#, A
IV Chord: D, F#, A   (1, 2, 3, 4, 5, 6, 7, 8)
V Chord: E, G#, B   **3 Sharps(#)**
VI Chord: F#, A#, C#
VII Chord: G#, C, D#

Key of "B-flat(b)"

I Chord: Bb, D, F
II Chord: C, E, G
III Chord: D, Gb, A   Bb, C, D, Eb, F, G, A, Bb
IV Chord: Eb, G, Bb   (1, 2, 3, 4, 5, 6, 7, 8)
V Chord: F, A, C   **2 Flats(b)**
VI Chord: G, B, D
VII Chord: A, Db, E

Key of "B"

I Chord: B, D#, F#
II Chord: C#, F, G#
III Chord: D#, G, A#   B, C#, D#, E, F#,G#, A# B
IV Chord: E, G#, B   (1, 2, 3, 4, 5, 6, 7, 8)
V Chord: F#, A#, C#   **5 Sharps(#)**
VI Chord: G#, C, D#
VII Chord: A#, D, F

Key of C

I Chord: C, E, G
II Chord: D, F#, A
III Chord: E, G#, B   C, D, E, F, G, A, B, C
IV Chord: F, A, C   (1, 2, 3, 4, 5, 6, 7, 8)
V Chord: G, B, D   **No Sharps(#)**
VI Chord: A, C#, E   **No Flats(b)**
VII Chord: B, D#, F#

Key of "C#" Major Scale of each Key

I Chord: C#, F, G#
II Chord: D#, G, A#
III Chord: F, A, C   C#, D#, F, F#, G#, A#, C, C#
IV Chord: F#, A#, C#   (1, 2, 3, 4, 5, 6, 7, 8)
V Chord: G#, C, D#   **5 Sharps(#)**
VI Chord: A#, D, F
VII Chord: C, E, G

Key of "D"

I Chord: D, F#, A
II Chord: E, G#, B
III Chord: F#, A#, C#   D, E, F#, G, A, B, C#, D
IV Chord: G, B, D   (1, 2, 3, 4, 5, 6, 7, 8)
V Chord: A, C#, E   **2 Sharps(#)**
VI Chord: B, D#, F#
VII Chord: C#, F, G#

Key of "Eb"

I Chord: Eb, G, Bb
II Chord: F, A, C

III Chord: G, B, D   Eb, F, G, Ab, Bb, C, D, Eb
IV Chord: Ab, C, Eb   (1, 2, 3, 4, 5, 6, 7, 8)
V Chord: Bb, D, F   **3 Flats(b)**
VI Chord: C, E, G
VII Chord: D, Gb, A

Key of "E"

I Chord: E, G#, B
II Chord: F#, A#, C#
III Chord: G#, C, D#   E, F#, G#, A, B, C#, D#, E
IV Chord: A, C#, E   (1, 2, 3, 4, 5, 6, 7, 8)
V Chord: B, D#, F#   **4 Sharps(#)**
VI Chord: C#, F, G#
VII Chord: D#, G, A#

Key of "F"   ## Major Scales

I Chord: F, A, C
II Chord: G, B, D
III Chord: A, Db, E   F, G, A, Bb, C, D, E, F
IV Chord: Bb, D, F   (1, 2, 3, 4, 5, 6, 7, 8)
V Chord: C, E, G   **1 Flat(b)**
VI Chord: D, Gb, A
VII Chord: E, Ab, B

Key of "Gb"

I Chord: Gb, Bb, Db
II Chord: Ab, C, Eb
III Chord: Bb, D, F   Gb, Ab, Bb, B, Db, Eb, F, Gb
IV Chord: B, Eb, Gb   (1, 2, 3, 4, 5, 6, 7, 8)
V Chord: Db, F, Ab   **5 Flats(b)**
VI Chord: Eb, G, Bb
VII Chord: F, A, C

Key of "G"

I Chord: G, B, D,
II Chord: A, C#, E
III Chord: B, D#, F#   G, A, B, C, D, E, F#, G
IV Chord: C, E, G   (1, 2, 3, 4, 5, 6, 7, 8)
V Chord: D, F#, A   **1 Sharp(#)**
VI Chord: E, G#, B
VII Chord: F#, A#, C#

Key of "Ab" (A-flat)

I Chord: Ab, C, Eb
II Chord: Bb, D, F
III Chord: C, E, G   Λb, Bb, C, Db, Eb, F, G, Ab
IV Chord: Db, F, Ab   (1, 2, 3, 4, 5, 6, 7, 8)
V Chord: Eb, G, Bb   **4 Flats(b)**
VI Chord: F, A, C
VII Chord: G, B, D

Glossary

ASCENDING: To play in the direction of the higher notes (right).

DESCENDING: To play in the direction of the lower notes (left).

CHORD: A combination of notes played simultaneously in harmonic tones with each other.

CHORUS: A repeating and most memorable part of a song.

INVERSION: An interchange of positions of notes, such as notes in a Chord and Chords in a song.

key (lower case): A lever pressed by a finger on a musical instrument such as a piano.

Key (upper case): A scale of notes consisting of chords which define the pitch at which a song will be played/sung.

LOWER/FLAT: An instruction to play the next ½-step or whole-step lower than a particular note.

RAISE/SHARP: An instruction to play the next ½-step or whole-step higherthan a particular note.

MAPPING: The act of organizing the Verse, Chorus, Bridge and band-solo in terms of positioning each aspect's position in a song.

MEASURE: The beats and notes lying between vertical lines on a musical staff; Relating to the meter or tempo of a song.

OCTAVES: Each interval of a group of 8 major-scale of notes and/or 12 Chromatic-scale of notes.

RELATIVE: Musical tones considered with respect to, and in relationship to each other.

ROOT: The "natural" first note of a scale and/or a chord, or which scale or chord gets its name.

SCALE: An ascending or descending series of musical tones proceeding in accordance with a specified scheme of intervals.

TEMPO: The speed at which a musical composition is to be played; the rate or rhythm of same.

TRANSPOSE: To write or perform a composition in a "Key" other than the one In which the composition was originally written.

TONE: A sound that has a distinct pitch, duration, loudness and quality.

INTERVALS: Difference in pitch between tones.

PITCH: The property of a musical tone that is determined by the frequency of the sound waves producing it: highness or lowness of sound.

Made in the USA
Monee, IL
22 December 2020